EXPECT MORE!

"For thirty-three years, Muffet McGraw coached our basketball team, achieving great success and taking women's basketball at Notre Dame and nationally to unprecedented heights. She has, in this insightful book, taken all of the lessons learned throughout her distinguished career and provided a guide to leadership and life that will be tremendously beneficial to rising women leaders as well as anyone committed to encouraging and empowering capable, confident women leaders."

Rev. John I. Jenkins, C.S.C.
President
University of Notre Dame

"Muffet McGraw's extraordinary success as a basketball coach earned her a richly deserved spot in the Naismith Memorial Basketball Hall of Fame, but for her, that success pales in comparison to her success in developing confident, empowered young women who are prepared to lead. Having worked closely with her for twelve years, I had the privilege of observing and learning much from McGraw that I now apply to my personal and professional life. I am thrilled that with the publication of *Expect More!* others will now get the opportunity to gain similar insights."

Jack Swarbrick
Vice President and James E. Rohr Director of Athletics
University of Notre Dame

"It is no surprise that this book would be titled *Expect More!* because that is exactly how Muffet McGraw coached and how she led the Notre Dame women's basketball program—powerfully, highly competitively, brilliantly, forcefully, and demandingly. She established a standard of excellence at Notre Dame and anything less than that was a disappointment and practically unacceptable. And that's why she is the best and loved by so many. She always expected more of us, and we tried our best to deliver. She sharpened my drive to be the best by setting the example in the way that she lived her life. I am a reflection of the values and lessons she instilled in me, and I will be forever grateful for her mentorship and guidance. I am strong, I am successful, and I am powerful because of her. I understand the importance of representation and opportunity, and I am fortunate to not only call Coach McGraw my mentor but also my friend."

Niele Ivey
Head Basketball Coach
University of Notre Dame

"Muffet McGraw emphatically and unapologetically declares the value and worth of girls and women everywhere. This book masterfully shines a spotlight on the biases, behaviors, laws, and stereotypes where inequality is bred and thrives. McGraw does more than declare that women should have an equal seat at the table; she challenges and empowers us all to pursue that seat for ourselves!"

Ruth Riley Hunter
University of Notre Dame Women's Basketball (1997–2001)
WNBA (2001–2014)

"I've always described the Notre Dame basketball program as 'servants to the game.' The Irish play basketball in ways that makes each player better with the details not found on the stat sheet. Muffet McGraw takes you on an intimate dive into how to lead your team in any arena of life: athletics, the classroom, or a corporate setting. *Expect More!* will empower you to lead with conviction and with a full heart."

Debbie Antonelli
College Basketball Analyst

EXPECT MORE!

DARE TO STAND UP AND STAND OUT

A GUIDE FOR WOMEN ON REACHING THEIR POTENTIAL

MUFFET McGRAW

AVE MARIA PRESS AVE Notre Dame, Indiana

Founded in 1865, Ave Maria Press is a ministry of the United States Province of Holy Cross.

www.avemariapress.com

Hardcover: ISBN-13 978-1-64680-068-1

E-book: ISBN-13 978-1-64680-069-8

Cover image © Getty Images / Andy Lyons / Staff.

Cover and text design by Brianna Dombo.

Printed and bound in the United States of America.

Library of Congress Cataloging-in-Publication Data
Names: McGraw, Muffet, author.
Title: Expect more! : dare to stand up and stand out / Muffet McGraw.
Description: Notre Dame : Ave Maria Press, [2021] | "A guide for women on reaching their potential"--Title page. | Audience: Grades 10-12 | Summary: "In this book, retired Notre Dame women's basketball coach Muffet McGraw shares a bold and timely message to all involved in the structures of groups, teams, businesses, and society: It's time for women to take a rightful and fair place in positions of leadership with confidence and an outward "swagger.""-- Provided by publisher.
Identifiers: LCCN 2020042994 (print) | LCCN 2020042995 (ebook) | ISBN 9781646800681 (Hardcover) | ISBN 9781646800698 (E-book)
Subjects: LCSH: Self-actualization (Psychology) in women--Juvenile literature. | Leadership in women--Juvenile literature. | Success--Juvenile literature.
Classification: LCC BF637.S4 M2397 2021 (print) | LCC BF637.S4 (ebook) | DDC 158.1082--dc23
LC record available at https://lccn.loc.gov/2020042994
LC ebook record available at https://lccn.loc.gov/2020042995

TO MATT,

for always believing in me, for making me laugh, and for being beside me every step of the way. If I could pick anyone in the world to share my life with it, I would still choose you.

TO ALL THE AMAZING WOMEN I HAVE BEEN BLESSED TO COACH,

thank you for being a part of my journey. I will treasure the memories we have made together and look forward to the ones that are still to come.

TO THE ONES I LEANED ON THE MOST,

the best assistant coaches in the business. Thank you for your hard work, your attention to detail, your unwavering support and loyalty, but most of all for your friendship. There are so many great memories that I will treasure forever.

CONTENTS

INTRODUCTION

I loved playing sports when I was a kid. But at the time—the late 1960s and early 1970s—organized sports were mostly for boys. I knew that girls weren't really supposed to play sports, but I never let it stop me.

My first coach in junior high basketball was a nun, so I did play for a woman coach right off the bat! I played high school basketball at Bishop Shanahan in West Chester, Pennsylvania, for Coach Jim Hetherington. We played in the afternoons; the boys played on Friday nights. They took busloads of fans to away games and we couldn't draw a crowd at home. I wondered why people didn't come and see us play back then and wondered the same thing for the next thirty years.

Title IX—the famous federal civil rights law that guaranteed equal opportunities in athletics to women—was passed in 1972, but it would be a long time before things ever got close to being equal.

I was on the first women's basketball team at Saint Joseph's University in Philadelphia in 1973–74. We did have a female coach—in fact three female coaches in four years—which was typical for college sports back then. The differences between the women's and men's teams were striking. We didn't have scholarships. We didn't have practice gear, sneakers, or a decent locker room. We sat in the bleachers and waited for both the men's varsity *and* men's junior varsity teams to finish practice before we could take the court. They chose when they would stop playing. Only then could we start our practice.

A small contingent of fans watched our games—mostly our parents and roommates. Occasionally, if we were lucky, our school newspaper would write an article about our team. The budget didn't allow us to take a bus to games so we had to drive in our own cars. Our schedule was limited to the geographic boundaries of Philadelphia.

I loved basketball through all of those challenges. I had played in games at the park growing up. Usually I was the only girl. When I got to St. Joe's, just having the opportunity to play was all I wanted—at least at first.

I was a sociology and criminal justice major in college. After I graduated I wanted to save the world, but I had no idea what that actually meant. There weren't a lot of jobs in sociology, so when a local high school coaching job opened, I thought, *what the heck, I'll give it a try*. After my first practice, I was completely consumed with coaching. This was definitely a passion I knew I had. I couldn't stop thinking about offenses and defenses. I loved doodling plays on napkins. I loved watching games. Of course, back then there were few female role models to draw from. So I watched the NBA and tried to bring back what they were doing in the men's game to the women's side.

When I got my first college head coaching job at Lehigh University in 1982 I also had to coach softball. None of the men's coaches were required to coach another sport but the women all did. I was so happy to get the basketball job that I didn't complain. I could have taken our administration to task based on the requirements of Title IX but since none of the other women's coaches protested I didn't want to make waves for them.

We did have our own gym at Lehigh, which was way ahead of most schools. I recall that the lighting in the gym was quite dark and without fail an opposing coach would come in and ask when we would be turning the rest of the lights on! I also had to mop the gym floor, set out the thirty-second clock (which used to sit in the corner of the court), and pay the referees. I admit that after some losses the refs may not have gotten their checks on time.

I was hired to coach at Notre Dame in 1987. Until that time, I had never lived away from the Philadelphia area for more than a few months. One thing did change for me when I came to Notre Dame: My sisters were always supportive of me but, for the first time, my brothers were proud to tell others that their sister was a basketball coach!

Things weren't perfect at Notre Dame right away. There were times when the men's team would fly to a game and we would have to bus to the same location. They ate at nice restaurants on the road and we ate fast food. Our coaches and staff were shoehorned into three offices so tiny that they were finally renovated into one medium-sized conference room. The men had a suite of offices for their staff.

Suffice it to say, I always expected more for my team and myself.

WHY I WROTE THIS BOOK

At my 2019 Final Four press conference, I was asked a question about hiring women on my staff and my response went viral. By the late 1990s—also due to regulations from Title IX—there was more equity in salaries for coaches in men's and women's sports. And male coaches swarmed to the women's sports. Coaching on the men's side was competitive and hard to break into and with more schools offering more women's sports, there were more opportunities for male coaches. Of course the opportunities for women to coach men's sports were nonexistent, so now we were not only competing with women for jobs but we had a new surplus of men to fight with too.

By 2019 I was well established as a coach. I had won two national championships at Notre Dame, the second in the previous season. I was confident enough to speak out on the absence of female leadership across the country in every field. As part of my answer to the reporter at the press conference, I advocated for more women in leadership in all areas, not just sports.

The response to my answer was amazing: about 95 percent of the comments were positive and only a few were chauvinistic or sexist ones. My words sparked a new dialogue about the topic of women in positions of leadership. *Expect More!* continues that conversation. There is so much that needs to change in this area. If you look around, you will see that despite studies extolling how beneficial it is to have a woman at the top of an organization, most women still have to fight just to find a place at the table.

I have written *Expect More!: Dare to Stand Up and Stand Out: A Guide for Women on Reaching Their*

Potential to encourage women—from school-age to those entering or in the midst of their careers—to not be satisfied with the status quo and to instead reach for the top in whatever organization and whatever field they find themselves, be it business, health care, politics, athletics, and more.

This book is also for fathers who are looking for ways to encourage and bolster the opportunities for their daughters in the same ways they have done for their sons. It is for coaches to read and to give to their players.

Finally, this book is for anyone—man or woman—who is or soon will be in an organization led by a woman. Women have the capacity to be great leaders in any sphere in society and we all play a role in making this possible. My hope is that relating my experiences in this book will be one more step in the long road toward encouraging more women to stand up and stand out.

1.

YOU CAN NEVER REST

There were twenty-two seconds left in the 2018 national semi-final game in Columbus, Ohio. We were up by five when University of Connecticut's team called a time-out. Our team had the attitude "we have this game won" and "we just have to hold on and we will be playing for a national championship." I was a bit more cautious, but by and large I shared my players' confidence. As any coach will tell you, having a five-point lead with twenty-two seconds left should be enough to win the game.

I gathered my team and told them two things: First, do not give up a three-pointer. "You can allow them a two-pointer, even a layup," I said. My thinking was that if we held them to two points, they would be forced to foul us and all we would have to do would be to make one free throw to put us up by four points, making it a two-possession game. The second thing I told them was a reminder that we only had one time-out left. "Don't use it unless you get really stuck." My thinking here was that if we got the ball in quickly after they scored, they would foul us immediately, and we would still have a time-out for an emergency.

Well, we went out on defense and a UConn player drove right to the basket heading toward a layup. Rather than let her score as we talked about, one of our defenders ran away from the girl she was guarding at the three-point line to help near the basket. The UConn player saw her open teammate and hit her with a pass and she connected for a three-pointer. In addition to that miscue, one of my players immediately called a time out. So we went zero-for-two in listening during our huddle.

After the time-out we had to inbound the ball on our sideline, right near our bench. This can be difficult to do, but we had worked on a play which involved setting a screen for the player who would come to receive the ball. Unfortunately, we didn't set a good screen and our player didn't come to meet the pass. Connecticut stole the ball, converted a layup, and just like that it was a tied game. We also turned the ball over again with a few seconds left but luckily UConn missed their final shot and the game went to overtime.

Some teams, having given up a big lead in the last few seconds, would have been so demoralized that they wouldn't have the persistence and toughness to win the game in overtime. And some coaches would have wanted to scream at their players, "How could you have done that?" or "I told you not to do that!" I recognized that we had just lost the momentum and my team was feeling despair during the break between regulation and overtime. The last thing they needed was for me to remind them of how they failed.

When I looked at them in the huddle, all of their heads were down. They all looked disappointed. Except for one player. She was angry that she didn't personally go get the ball and make them foul her instead of allowing someone else to make a bad decision. I took one look at Arike Ogunbowale and knew that if the game came down to a last-second shot, she would be the one to take it.

Arike Ogunbowale makes the game-winning shot in the 2018 semi-final game.

And the rest is history. Arike hit the game-winner with one second remaining to send us on to the championship game. We managed to turn failure into success, but I was not about to let go of the lesson of what we did at the end of regulation and move on just yet. It was a teaching moment and the lesson was . . . *you can never rest.* With a five-point lead and only twenty-two seconds left, we should have won that game in regulation but we took our foot off the gas for a few seconds and lost our focus. It almost cost us the game.

NO LEAD IS SAFE

As a coach, I never felt like a lead was safe. Reporters would always ask me after the game when I knew that we would win and I would usually answer, "When I cleared the bench with thirty seconds left and we were up by fifteen!" It's a coach's job to be sure that no one gets overconfident. It's the same for anyone pursuing leadership or in a leadership position. Don't assume anything is going to be handed to you. If you are a woman, there is a good chance it will actually be more difficult to achieve and maintain success. You can't ever play it safe or play not to lose. You have to be aggressive and keep attacking.

Often during a season, if your team gets off to a good start and wins a few games, everyone begins to look ahead and forgets the task at hand. Or, even if they focus on the current game, they may think they can turn it on and play well in the fourth quarter while coasting at the beginning. There are so many ways to lose a game or make the score closer than it should be when the team is looking beyond what is happening now. When players and coaches forget the task at hand, it gives the other team the confidence to stay in the game. Underdog teams love when this happens. It's always easier to play as an underdog when there's no pressure and everyone expects you to lose. The pressure is always on the higher-ranked team. The way to alleviate the pressure is to stay focused and not look ahead.

I never talked to the team about winning a game. Our pregame talks involved our keys to being successful,

not a score or the outcome. You can't focus on the final score, because that really isn't something you can control. In basketball, you can't *make* the ball go in the basket. Certainly, practicing shooting helps, but there are certain days when you just can't make a shot. And suddenly the bad shooting is contagious among your teammates. Everyone is looking for someone else to make a big play.

When this happens I think it's always important to stay in the moment. Take care of this one possession— offensive and defensive—at a time. One stop, one score. You can't try to protect a lead by hoping something good happens. You can't hope the other team misses. You have to set the tone early and let the other team know that you are prepared to battle for the entire forty minutes of the game. This philosophy is true for any part of life. You can't take for granted that things will work out on their own. You have to be the one to achieve your own success.

I had so many great players at Notre Dame, but the ones who were really special were those who never took a possession off. They never rested. They came at the other team at every opportunity. They wanted to wear the opponent down. If we were up by ten points, they would get in the huddle and say, "Let's get up by twenty." Not only would they never rest, they wouldn't let their teammates rest either.

No one is going to give you anything as you reach for your success. The only thing you can control is *you*. This means you can control your own effort, your own focus, your own discipline, and everything you think and believe. You can control your own attitude. You can remain positive. It's up to you to figure out what it takes to get to the lead and to stay in front. I love the quote of Australian author Sara Henderson who said, "Don't wait for a light to appear at the end of the tunnel, stride down there and light the bloody thing yourself!"

DON'T RELAX AFTER YOU TASTE SUCCESS

Don't be satisfied because someone has told you that you are talented or because things have always gone well for you. Always look for the other shoe to drop. Really, you can never relax when you are trying to reach the top. I never do. I looked at every game as a potential loss. We always talked about a team's strengths, even if they were having a bad season or were at the bottom of our league standings. I believed that every team, no matter how much they were struggling, had a game in them in which they could rise to the challenge and win. Look at the strengths of those you are competing with for a job or in school or for a place on a team. Expect everyone to give you a fight.

How do you keep from being complacent? In a game situation, it's important to stay loose. This is something I have never been good at. When you are competing, there is no time for negative self-talk. You have to stay loose *and* confident. If you are a team leader, the best player, or the coach—and particularly when you are the coach—staying calm under pressure lets the others know that everything is under control. A way to put this into practice is to take a deep breath. Assure yourself that you are fine, and then give that same message to your team. You are able to handle this situation and so can the others.

People will often tell you that you are on your way to success. Listen to the compliment, but then push it aside. Although I agree it's great to be on the right track for your course in life, people will overtake you or literally run by you if you just stay in the same place. At Notre Dame, we rarely lost to an unranked team. Some of that was because our leaders in the locker room did not allow anyone to become complacent. Our coaches didn't become complacent either. We scouted every opponent the same way. We never looked past anyone. Neither should you! If you aren't moving forward, you are falling behind!

WHAT ABOUT FAILURE?

In every game there are moments when you succeed and other moments when you fail. In fact, in sports there are a lot of opportunities to fail. This is one of the great things about sports. Failure is an opportunity to improve and do better. You can use failure as a lesson for improving in other areas of your life too.

We were fortunate to have great success in our program over my thirty-three seasons as coach, but my final season in 2019–20 was a series of learning experiences. We had a losing record and a lot of failures. When you do fail you can't wallow in your misery. You need to look objectively at what happened and figure out what you can learn from it. And you need to act.

Looking at our losing season as a whole, I wonder if I should have changed our expectations or at least set some reasonable weekly goals. Our program was coming off of back-to-back appearances in the national championship game. But if the current team wasn't capable of winning the conference championship, maybe that shouldn't have been a goal. We could have adjusted our goals game by game so the team didn't constantly feel the strain of failing. We did edit the game film to show the players only highlights, but there usually weren't enough good plays to build confidence. Sometimes we would

show film of good execution even when our players missed a shot, just so they could feel good about something.

Our method was different from 2011 to 2019, when we went to seven Final Fours. We had some great teams, though occasionally we would have games in which we didn't play to our potential, even when we won. What the players on those teams remember the most and still talk about today is the practices following those games when we didn't play well. It's safe to say we didn't watch our highlights after those games.

Winning allows you to be a little more critical. I liked to follow the old saying that "what you allow is what will continue," so we would show those teams examples of plays with poor effort or execution. I needed to let the team know that their subpar performance was not acceptable.

The 2019–20 team felt the burden of the program's history of winning. They didn't want to be the Notre Dame team to stop our streak of twenty-four consecutive NCAA tournament appearances. The team was motivated to fix its failures, but all of the pressure caused an opposite effect. We played not to lose close games. We lost our confidence early in games and didn't have an All-American to lead us like we had had in the past. I hate to lose more than I like to win. Having a losing season was agony for me. The team was young and inexperienced and it took us a long time to find our way.

FIXING FAILURE

I've heard about the advantage of people failing early and failing often. Thomas Edison once said he found 999 ways *not* to make electricity. I felt like I learned 999 ways *not* to win a game. What can you learn from when you fail?

I always asked myself tough questions related to where we went wrong. Was it the game plan? Was it the execution of the game plan? Was it our communication as coaches? As the head coach or a leader in any situation, it's important that you are willing to be accountable and take full responsibility for failure.

I had to make a lot of decisions from the sideline during a game. I liked to hear from my assistants during the game, especially during time-outs. But I had guidelines for *what* I wanted to hear from my assistants. For example, it didn't help me if one of my coaches told me "Hey, the zone defense isn't working" or "So and so isn't having a good night." Really? We could all see those things! It's always easy to state the problem or to blame someone for what is going wrong. During a game, I wasn't looking for comments from Captain Obvious. I wanted suggestions for how to fix the problems.

I liked when my assistants asked me questions such as, "Should we try to play man-to-man?" or "Should we make a substitution here?" Whatever the problem is, it is the leader's job to fix it. Laying blame might make you feel better at first, but in the long run blaming someone else doesn't help anyone. You won't solve the immediate problem and you will lose your team.

Besides correcting problems in real time, you also have to have a way to fix failures after they occur. Imagine you didn't get a job or promotion you wanted or got cut from a team or lost a starting spot in the lineup. After experiences like these, it's important to do a more detailed evaluation of what went wrong and how you can improve.

As head coach, I would begin our postgame evaluation by first stating what went well and how we could improve on those successes. I would also make sure to compliment my staff on the job they did well while at the same time mentioning ways they could improve. I would often ask the team "What do you think we did well?" I loved to have input from the group and asking questions is the best way to get it.

We always tried to show the team highlights after games—even after losses (at least sometimes!)—to show how they had executed the game plan and did what we had worked on in practice. For example, we had defensive film clips showing how they guarded someone exactly as we practiced. And we always tried to show offensive baskets that came off assists from another player to further ingrain the unselfish team philosophy.

Whether we were having a good season or a bad one, we approached our evaluations in the same way. I never critiqued the players until after I had watched the film of the game. You probably won't be surprised to hear that it was much easier to deliver the game evaluation after we won. The players were much more receptive too!

We held individual meetings with each player after the season as well as a final team meeting with everyone together. During these individual meetings, we talked about what each player did well and what she could improve on in the offseason. We also talked about their goals for the next season and gave them concrete ideas on ways they could work on them. It's easier in sports to quantify success than in other businesses. In sports, we can look at statistics and especially wins and losses, but even those don't tell a player whether she has improved or not. You can play well and lose and you can play poorly and win. You need to have personal standards that you hold yourself to.

Standards for success are not always tangible. As a leader, it was my job to tell each player and each assistant coach what expectations I had for them. To be clearer, I had to tell them exactly what their roles were on the team. For example, I would give each player three or four things to be responsible for, such as, being in the top three in rebounding, averaging a double-double (meaning double digits in two important statistical categories), leading the team in steals, or getting to the free throw line the most. Each player had specific things she was responsible for and I told them at a team meeting so that everyone knew everyone else's roles and what was expected of each person on the team. I also set up the same type of expectations for my coaches.

Having clear expectations is one of the key ways to fix failures and have success. In the bestselling business book *Good to Great*, author Jim Collins wrote about how it wasn't enough to get the right people on the bus, you have to also get them in the right seat. In other words, as a leader, you have to assemble the right team and then assign them roles they can accomplish. Sometimes I would set the bar a little lower in terms of individual expectations for freshmen so that they could see some tangible success early on. As the players got older, I would demand more from them. I never lowered the team expectations and made it a point to celebrate when they did accomplish their goals.

ALWAYS EXPECT MORE

My coaching philosophy could be summed up in two words: *expect more*. I was never happy with the status quo. Even when we won a game, I looked at the game film with just as much intent in order to find the things we could do better. You better believe that after the national semi-final game where we squandered a five-point lead at the end of regulation, we talked again and

Brianna Turner celebrates the 2018 national championship.

again about how important it is not to succumb to the pressure of the game and to lean on the discipline it takes to play the right way.

In keeping with my philosophy, I congratulated the players on how well they played in some areas, but always let them know there were other areas where they could improve. "You had twenty points?" I might say, "Great, but I expected you to get more than four rebounds."

Most people don't know how much more they have inside of them that is still untapped. A leader is needed to pull out the extra potential. You do have to be careful that the person you are pushing to be great may not want to be. Some people are easily satisfied. A player once said to me, "Coach, you are never satisfied." I took it as a compliment, but soon realized she didn't mean it that way. I told her that I would never settle for less. I always expect more. Why wouldn't she? I was reminded of the saying "You can never push someone up the ladder unless they are willing to climb."

2.

BRING YOUR SWAGGER

My teams used to be described as "businesslike" or "possessing a blue-collar work ethic." And I liked those descriptions. I never liked seeing players over-celebrate and call attention to themselves on the court or field. I wanted players who showed class and kept the attention off themselves personally and focused only on the team.

Skylar Diggins changed how I felt about players calling attention to themselves and displaying swagger. Skylar was a local player from South Bend's Washington High School who grew up playing basketball at a gym supervised by her stepfather. She came to Notre Dame in 2009 with a lot of confidence. Before every game, while I sat by myself in the locker room stressing out, Sky (along with her teammate Devereaux Peters) would pass by me on the way to the court, look me in the eyes, and say "We got you!" I can't tell you how much I loved hearing those words. They made me smile and they helped me to relax.

Skylar Diggins

Skylar Diggins had that kind of confidence. She believed in herself and made you believe right along with her. I had always loved when players celebrated for each other, but I wasn't quite sold on them beating their chests and putting the spotlight squarely on themselves. But Skylar changed that for me too. I asked myself, *why shouldn't we celebrate our own success which naturally has a huge impact on the success of our team?* And Skylar's celebrations were always related to our team's success. She was just as happy to rejoice over a teammate's basket as one of her own.

Perhaps it was the stereotype of how women should play and how women should act that was keeping me from watching and accepting their exuberance. I liked to see joy on the faces of my players. After all, men have been displaying swagger on the basketball court and in other sports for years. Why aren't women encouraged to visibly celebrate and play with swagger? Outside of the sport's arena, the same has been true. Men typically have a bigger presence in the workplace, boldly making themselves known. Women have more often shrunk into the background, doing their jobs well without drawing outward attention to themselves.

Because of Skylar, I began to consciously recruit players who demonstrated plenty of outward confidence. Skylar Diggins paved the way for Arike Ogunbowale. By the time Arike arrived, I was fully embracing players with swagger.

SPORTS BREED CONFIDENCE

Sports teach many lessons that can be applied to anyone's life, such as, discipline, a good work ethic, resilience, grit, and confidence. Sports are so competitive that the only way for a person to succeed is to work harder than others. In sports there are no handouts. No one is going to feel sorry for you and move you along. No one competing with you is going to care about a problem you have in shooting the ball or shuffling your feet on defense that might be holding you back from making a team or getting more playing time. In a competitive situation, most people are only concerned with themselves.

More than anything else, sports breed confidence. You can't have success without confidence. And you can't have swagger unless you are successful at what you do.

Confidence comes from within. It is a firm trust that you can rely on. It comes from knowing you can do something because you've done it before. Not necessarily at game time (or exam time or interview time) but in your preparation. Confidence also comes from failing, recognizing what you did wrong, and fixing it.

Today, many people have a false sense of confidence. This could be from the way they grew up as kids. Parents nowadays spend so much time praising their kids (especially in sports) and telling them how good they are that when something goes wrong, then it is never their own fault. Everyone—kids included—needs to hear the truth. Parents don't have to be brutally honest with younger kids, but they still need to be truthful with them. Kids know instinctively when they are being lied to; they know their position on the team in terms of their ability compared to the ability of others.

This doesn't mean that each person on a team or part of a group can't have success. There are other measures of success besides innate ability. Often parents don't have the right perspective when it comes to speaking to their kids about their performance in sports. They watch the game and tell their child: "I want you to play more" and "I want you to shoot more." And if those things don't happen it becomes the coach's fault. Resentment builds between the coach and player. This attitude impacts others on the team too. Parents need to readjust their view. Parents should praise their children for their effort, dedication, and improvement. They should notice the way their daughter interacts with her teammates and how she listens to her coaches.

Everyone can't be the MVP and everyone doesn't get to be the hero at the end of the game. But everyone's job on a team is important. Just because you aren't the star player doesn't mean you aren't important. Remember, it's the coach's job to make sure everyone on their team feels like they are a vital part of the success of the team. Even the last player on the bench has a role to play.

In 2015 we were in the Final Four playing South Carolina in the national semifinals. We were up by one with nineteen seconds left in regulation when I inserted Hannah Huffman into the game to guard South Carolina's best player. Hannah was a "defensive specialist." Her role on the team was a complimentary one. She did the little, intangible things that didn't get noticed. The announcers on television were

Hannah Huffman

shocked when I put Hannah in at such a crucial point. I would not have asked her to score the winning basket, but I had all the confidence that Hannah could defend. I trusted her to get the most important defensive stop of the season and she did just that! I will never forget watching Hannah celebrate after the game. She raised her arms, hugged her teammates, and thumped her chest. It was pure joy! She was rejoicing in the fact that she came through for her team. It was so fun to watch.

Think about how this lesson applies to family life and in business. You may have noticed mothers, fathers, and older children out front of their house in the fall raking leaves. And in the midst of this work, a toddler holds a miniature rake and imitates what the others are doing. Is the toddler's actual raking really necessary to getting the job done? Probably not. But she is learning a lesson that she is important and that she contributes to the work of the family.

When you are leading any business it's important to let everyone know they are a vital part of the organization. It's important to recognize and thank those who take care of the office, make coffee in the morning, and all others who are responsible for the small details that make everyone's job easier and the business more successful. For example, have you ever considered the importance of a receptionist? When people come to your office or call in by phone, the receptionist is the first person who sets the tone through attitude and demeanor. What an important position in any company!

I would often have meetings with everyone that touched my team in any way—from administrative assistants to marketing, sports information, and academic advisers—and just take some time to listen to them tell me how things were going and how I might help them. All anyone really wants is to feel like they are part of the organization. When a leader provides each member of the team a sense of belonging, an organization will flourish. When people feel appreciated and part of a team, they will do a better job.

In his bestselling book *The Culture Code: The Secrets of Highly Successful Groups*, Notre Dame graduate Daniel Coyle wrote of an experiment that was conducted at a call center in India for new employees. There were three control groups. The first group received a standard orientation. The second group received the same orientation but also got to spend an hour talking with current employees and received a shirt with the company's logo on the front. The third group had the same orientation as the second group, but their shirts also had the employee's own name printed on the back. After seven months on the job, those in the third group were 250 percent more likely to be still employed in the organization than those in the other groups. It is amazing what simple gestures of making people feel wanted and valuable can do for your team!

WHAT'S WRONG WITH WOMEN HAVING SWAGGER?

Showing outward emotion wasn't really a thing among any athletes until the 1960s. Prior to that, for the most part, players kept their head down and really didn't display much emotion when they competed. When the New York Yankees' Joe DiMaggio kicked at the dirt in anger after making an out in the 1947 World Series, the press was shocked that such a great player would let his emotions be seen by the public. That all changed when heavyweight boxer Muhammad Ali came on the scene. He had no problem drawing attention to himself. His famous line, which he shouted over and over after winning a fight, was "I am the greatest!" Soon other athletes were following his lead and showing their joy for playing a game with very visible swagger.

I should say many *men* athletes displayed swagger. Not so for women athletes. Then, in 1999 at the women's World Cup soccer finals at the Pasadena Rose Bowl, a United States player, Brandi Chastain, kicked the game-winning goal in the penalty shootout. What happened next was something people had seen men do all the time, but never a woman. Brandi fell to her knees, clenched her fists, and extended her arms over her head in celebration. She also tore off her jersey and continued to celebrate in her sports bra! The public was divided about her actions. Some were shocked that a woman would draw that kind of attention to herself. By the next season, it was a penalty for men and women to remove their shirts in celebration.

Why does the public seem to tolerate men showing swagger, and not women? There are stereotypes that still persist for how many people believe that women should act. More recently, at the 2018 US Open, tennis

In 2018 tennis champion Serena Williams made headlines for arguing with the chair umpire during her match.

champion Serena Williams got into an argument with the chair umpire who accused Serena of taking illegal signs from her coach who was sitting in the stands. Tensions grew throughout the match as Serena often yelled and pointed her finger at the official. The incident attracted worldwide attention and distracted from the young player, Naomi Osaka, who upset Serena to win the match. Why so much attention on Serena's actions? Hadn't we witnessed men argue with officials and never receive any scrutiny? You've probably seen many video clips of baseball managers going nose to nose with umpires. You probably never saw the same clips discussed in terms of the appropriateness of the demeanor of the men involved.

Where do the different expectations of how women and men play the game come from? Think of it this way: We are only a generation removed from when girls had to play basketball wearing skirts and bloomers. When I was in seventh grade, a priest came into the classroom and told us that our Catholic school was going to have its first girls' basketball team. He asked who was interested. My hand shot up. I had already been playing for years at the local park, the only girl playing five-on-five basketball with nine other guys. At the park, I let my play speak for itself. There were no referees on the playground. The ball was either in bounds or out. We decided who had knocked it out. We called our own fouls.

But when I first played organized basketball in seventh grade, not only did we have to wear the skirts and bloomers, we had to play a "less taxing" version of basketball that was only for females. Instead of five-on-five, we played six-on-six. Two players permanently played offense, two permanently played on the defensive side, and two other rovers were permitted to cross into both half-court zones. I presume the men in charge didn't think we had enough energy and stamina to play real basketball. Did they think childbirth was a pain-free experience? Did they think running up and down the court might make us faint?

DIFFERENCES IN MEN AND WOMEN COACHES

I've also seen a lot of visibly emotional men coaching basketball, both men's and women's basketball. They are often disheveled and enraged on the sidelines. They rant and rave at the referees. Why is this only acceptable for men? Women coaches are supposed to have a quiet confidence, but men can be demonstratively confident. I never once had to have my assistant coaches hold me

Geno Auriemma

back from going onto the court to complain about a referee's call. Yet Geno Auriemma, the UConn coach, has charged onto the playing floor many times, and the media just chalks it up to his letting the officials know he didn't like a certain call. I don't recall a single time when Geno was called for a technical foul in a game against Notre Dame, but when Baylor coach Kim Mulkey was similarly enraged by a referee's call when we played them in the 2014 regional final, she was given a technical. Take a look the next time you watch a women's game featuring a man and woman coaching on different sides. Notice what happens when each goes outside the prescribed coaching box. Will the woman be told to get back inside the box? Will the man even be reprimanded?

Female coaches at all levels of basketball are judged by a different standard than their male counterparts. Men seem to get away with a lot more—whether it's in their tone of voice, their language, or their demeanor— than women do. Men are allowed to be angry; women are not.

I think players are willing to take harsher behavior from a male coach than they are from a woman coach. There are some men coaches who say things to their players in ways and using words that I could never imagine. If I had spoken that way, I would have been in the athletic director's office facing a complaint about verbal abuse. Women players expect that their male coach is going to talk to them in a way that a female coach may not. This is a disadvantage for a woman coach who may have to hold back her words rather than be brutally honest with a player. When a woman coach critiques a player harshly, the player wonders whether or not the coach "likes her." She probably wouldn't take a male coach's criticism in the same way. So the issue goes both ways: It's up to the woman leader to be able to speak honestly in whatever way she is most comfortable and it's up to the person working under the woman leader to not filter the advice in a different way than she or he would if it came from a man.

It's also up to those in charge of the game or the larger structures, like of the game of basketball itself. I was happy to see that a male coach in a recent Final Four was reprimanded and penalized by the women's basketball committee for his language and demeanor on the sideline. It's good to know that people are watching and standing up for the integrity of our game. But what is happening when they are not watching?

OVERCOMING THE STEREOTYPES

In sports, women are often held back from full participation or pigeonholed by stereotypes. Sometimes men don't even realize how tradition or choices made by leadership prevent women from participating. For instance, I am an avid golfer and enjoy playing. Two incidents happened to me at Notre Dame concerning golf that left me shaking my head.

The first occurred when I played in a charity event to support the football team. There were about 287 men and only a few women, so I felt I had a good chance to win a prize or two. There were contests for longest drive, lowest score, and so on. But the contests were only open to men. I watched the men's winners receive prizes such as new drivers, new putters, and buckets of golf balls. I did receive a participatory prize (ugh), but instead of it being something to do with golf, it was a container of bubble bath! A few years later, the NFL Players Association had a golf outing at Notre Dame. I got a call to see if I would like to participate. I was pretty excited until the officials told me that they wanted me to sit at the third hole and determine which balls were hit closest to the hole. And they added: "Could you wear a short skirt?" I declined.

When women can be more themselves and show their swagger whenever they like, there is a better chance that these types of stereotypes will disappear. I think again about Skylar Diggins. When she left Notre Dame for the WNBA in 2013, she also

Jay-Z and Skylar Diggins

did something else. She was the first woman to sign with Jay-Z's Roc Nation sports agency. For the first time, a woman basketball player's fame transcended the game. Sky's cool, take-no-prisoners attitude from the basketball court—her swagger—has made her one of the most recognizable athletes in the world.

The attitude of swagger I learned from Skylar changed me in another way as a coach. Women's coaches were expected to be compassionate and empathetic. I've never been compassionate *or* empathetic. But I tried to fit into that mold before learning to be more myself. It's a shame that we are forced into those roles as women. It's a shame that if you are a female boss you are expected to treat your staff differently than a male boss would.

Men are expected to be driven and ambitious while women are not. Women are expected to be "good sports" and to act as if we don't care much if we win or lose. It's supposed to be enough for us to be lucky enough to be playing the game. Again, that's not me. I've always been driven and competitive. I've always wanted to win. I don't feel the need to apologize for those feelings. In fact, women need to learn from the time they are young girls that it is okay to want to be the best and to aim just as high or higher than men. It's okay to compete and go out and get what you want. It's good to know that, as a woman, you can play with swagger.

3.

ASSUME YOU ARE THE BEST

When my son Murphy was growing up I was amazed at how he would sound like the world's leading authority on virtually everything. Boys, in general, are supremely confident. Are they born like that, or are we somehow raising them that way? Do we treat our sons differently than we treat our daughters? Do we praise our daughters whenever they are aggressive, intense, or competitive? Or do we just tell them that they "look nice"?

It's time we spend more time telling our daughters how smart they are instead of just how pretty they are. As girls get better grades in math and science than boys at all grade levels, there is no reason there should not be more female engineers, scientists, and doctors than men. Right? Sometimes it takes more than a subtle push to steer women in directions different than they might have considered. It's up to we who lead to strongly encourage and challenge women along paths they might never seriously consider.

In the book *Confidence Code: The Science and Art of Self-Assurance—What Women Should Know*, authors Katty Kay and Claire Shipman present data that a girl's confidence peaks at age nine and doesn't really return to that same level until she is in her twenties. What happens in between? What makes girls stop believing in themselves during their teen years? How many times in class is a question asked and girls are hesitant to raise their hands even though they know the answer? When someone asks how to attack a problem, why do girls wait for boys to answer first?

Women need to take more risks and stop caring so much about what other people think. Eleanor Roosevelt said, "Do what you feel in your heart to be right—for you'll be criticized anyway." Women care way too much about what others think of them.

FIND YOUR VOICE

As a coach, I liked to ask a lot of questions. I asked questions during film sessions and at practice. I asked questions of the players on the bench during games. A lot of times when I asked questions I would hear crickets as a

reply, especially from the younger players. But eventually, after continuing to ask and sometimes pointedly calling out players by name to respond, they would begin to feel comfortable and use their voices.

Why ask so many questions? I found that most people would rather critique themselves than have someone else do it for them. As a leader, before you tell someone what they should have done, ask them what they were thinking about when they acted as they did. Ask them what else they could have done in that situation if they had the chance to do it over.

When the team watched film, we would stop it often in certain situations and ask the players what they

thought should happen next. "Did you see the open player? What were you thinking when you didn't pass her the
ball?" I had to make the point that the question "What
were you thinking?" is not a rhetorical question, nor
should it have negative consequences. I really wanted
to know. Usually I found out that they weren't thinking
at all. This told me that, as coaches, we needed to do a
better job of getting our players to "think the game." This
could only be improved when they watched the game
either sitting on the bench or later from film, listened
to coaches and team leaders, learned from what they
observed and heard, and then put it all into practice.

I asked players questions during the game because
they had a good view of what was going on. They were
the ones actually playing. Asking them questions when
they came to the bench kept them engaged. I also asked
the players questions at halftime. "What are you seeing on the court? What are some problem areas for our
team? What areas of our strength are we not taking
advantage of? Is there a mismatch between one of our
players and one of theirs that we could be exploiting?" In
an early time-out in the game I would ask specific questions such as, "How are they handling the ball screens?"
I imagined the freshmen were thinking to themselves,
"Dang, don't you know, Coach?"

At practice, I would pose open-ended questions that required players to think even more. I asked things such as, "What did you think about playing that type of defense?" or "What did you like better on our ball screen defense, a big hedge on the screen or a soft hedge?" What I was trying to do was to get the players to see that their voices would be heard. I wanted them to know that I was listening to what they had to say and that I was interested in their opinions. Doing that meant that sometimes I would get three different answers to the same question. But when that happened it would lead to even more discussion. Sometimes when we were working on end-of-the-game situations at practice I just listened in to the huddle and let the players decide what play to run. I especially wanted our captains to have a chance to lead.

Bottom line, the reason for all these questions was to build the confidence of the players. They were so happy when they answered a question correctly or when I took and used one of their suggestions. It was also a great way to get buy-in from the team. If everyone said a 2-3 zone defense worked really well against the scout team in practice and they would like to play it in the game, more power to them! They would have more confidence playing a 2-3 zone if it was their idea.

BE DECISIVE AND
BELIEVE IN YOURSELF

Asking questions and listening to answers is a good part of the formula of success for a leader in any situation. Most people—especially women—are easily intimidated and tend to hang back and hesitate to answer questions at first. In general, people hate to be wrong and are really hard on themselves if they misspeak and give a wrong answer. At Notre Dame, I had a lot of perfectionists on my teams. They really wanted to be right *every time*. They worked hard and they were never satisfied. Perfectionists expect a lot from themselves and feel more pressure to perform because they judge themselves so critically. This is ironic because it is their desire for perfection that makes them so good, but that desire is also their downfall because they can never attain the perfection they are seeking. This creates a lot of stress and anxiety which affects their performance.

Women tend to ruminate over their mistakes, whereas men can put them in their rearview mirror and move on. Women too often take responsibility for what goes wrong. And even when we do succeed, we are reluctant to take praise. When you tell a woman that she did a good job, the first thing she does is give credit to others:

her teammates, coworkers, classmates, or friends. Everyone but herself. When you tell a man that he did a good job, do you know what he says? He says, "Thank you." We need to learn how to just say thank you.

Also, women, in general, never assume that their way is the best. We want to have all the information at hand before we move forward. We want to be right! But I suggest we change our mindset and be more willing to be more spontaneous and answer first, even if we are wrong. We can always learn from our errors.

When I asked my players at our year-end meeting to evaluate what they did well during the season, their list was always a short one with plenty of caveats, such as, "I did well most of the time" or "I got a little better." They

Marina Mabrey

seemed to forget that making 50 percent of their shots is terrific. All they could focus on was that they missed the other 50 percent.

Women take criticism so personally but can't take compliments the same way. We walk a fine line between being confident and not too confident lest we be accused of being arrogant. We need to speak up for ourselves, but not too loudly because we are supposed to be humble. We should be proud of our success, but not brag because we are supposed to be team players. It's truly exhausting when you think about it!

Our best players were the ones who could fail and move on from it. I remember a reporter asking Arike Ogunbowale (below) how she felt at halftime of the Connecticut semi-final game because she was something like

0-for-10 shooting at that point. She was shocked to hear she had missed ten shots and said she just assumed that in the second half they would all go in. Great players put their mistakes aside and keep taking chances. They never stop shooting even if they haven't made many.

Really, most successful people never change their mindset. They assume the next shot will go in, the next idea will be accepted, the next project will secure more sales, and on and on. They are usually more surprised when they don't have success than when things go their way. It takes confidence to act this way. It's great to know that your coaches, supervisors, teammates, and coworkers believe in you, but it always comes down to how much you believe in yourself.

DON'T BE AFRAID TO LEAD

What fascinates me about leadership is how different so many leaders are. There are introverts and extroverts who lead. There are leaders who listen more than they talk and others who talk more than they listen. And they can all be successful. We often hear the phrase "leading by example." I would tell my team that leading by example is expected. That is something everyone has to do. But that's not real leadership. Real leadership is not being afraid to use your voice. You have to be able to go out

and say clearly, "This is what I want," and not think too much about how others will react to your words.

Often, women are hesitant to step up and lead with their voices and I think a lot of it has to do with wanting to be liked. I always ask my team captains, "Do you want to win or do you want to be liked?" because most times you can't have it both ways. In basketball, there are times when a leader will need to get on her teammates for their lack of hustle or focus. A leader will need to dish out some tough love in order to let someone know that she isn't doing what needs to be done on the court. Team leaders can't worry about hurting someone's feelings when they are in the middle of the game. They can't worry about whether or not their criticism of a teammate will carry over to after the game and cause some hurt feelings. When you play on a team or are part of any work group, there are certain expectations that everyone needs to live up to. A leader has to have the confidence to tell others that they aren't meeting the group's expectations. She also, of course, has to make sure that she is living up to those same standards.

Being decisive is another important trait for a leader. Why do women think they can't handle that kind of pressure? I think one of the reasons is that women imagine they have to overthink each decision before choosing an option and proceeding. That's not really true. One good thing about coaching basketball is that a time-out is thirty seconds to two minutes in length so it's really hard to overthink in that short amount of time. But even if your field is different from sports, don't let indecisiveness hamper your ability to lead. You have to be willing to take a risk and take a chance on your plan. Certainly, you will get input from your trusted staff before you make a decision. And then all it takes is to make a decision and go from there. Sometimes your decision will work out. Sometimes it won't. If it doesn't, learn from your mistake and move on. Don't dwell on it. Never lose your will to take a risk.

TAKING RISKS IS HOW YOU GROW

Women tend to think that everything has to be perfect before they make a decision. If there is a job opening and there are six qualifications needed and a woman meets five of the six, she dismisses herself as a candidate. Oppositely, if a man has only two of the qualifications for the same job he thinks "I can learn the rest after I'm hired." Men just assume they are the best candidate for any job. And if for whatever reason the man is not hired, he just chalks it up as someone else's fault. It certainly wasn't his fault! Women are more likely to take a rejection personally and assume they just didn't have the right credentials.

There are other differences between the way men and women approach opportunities. When a job opens up, men immediately pick up the phone. They call everyone on their contact list to see who they know who can help them get the job. Their resume is always up to date and ready to go. Not only that, it's amazing what men take personal credit for. They aren't afraid of taking credit for team accomplishments. Men are also really good at talking themselves up. They seem to always start a sentence with "I." Women start sentences with "We."

Women overthink things and try to look at every angle. By the time they are finally ready to apply, the moment has passed, and the process is closed.

An athletic director from another school with a good women's basketball program called me when he was interviewing for a head coach after the position had just opened up. He told me that he was surprised by the number of men who had already contacted him to let him know that they were the best candidate. What also surprised him was that he had texted one of the female assistants at his school and told her he was interested in talking with her about the job. After twenty-four hours he still had not heard back from her. I know what she was doing. She was checking the boxes of the experience she *didn't* have. She was talking with her friends and family and stressing out about all the reasons she was *not* ready for the job. Hint: no one will ever be totally ready.

Wouldn't it be great if women treated themselves like they treat their friends when those friends have an opportunity to be promoted or to take a new job? We encourage our friends and tell them how ready they are, how perfect the fit is, and how successful they will be after they are hired. But when it's for ourselves, we automatically think of all the reasons why we aren't meant for the job.

Women worry about so many things. We worry about what our current boss will think if it becomes known we applied for another job. Or we worry about whether our current boss's willingness to recommend us for another job is because he or she wants us to leave. Again, exhausting.

It used to be that almost 100 percent of coaches in women's basketball were women. Today, only about 42 percent of coaches are women. Why? The salaries grew. So we saw a lot of men coming over to women's sports. They either couldn't get a job in men's basketball or the process would take too long with too many dues for them to pay. But on the women's side they could walk in and be a head coach. With men, you also see recycled coaches. They get fired from one job and move on to another. But with women, it's very difficult to come back and get another job after being fired. Also, schools are reluctant to hire another woman to coach after one fails. A lot of times an athletic director will say, "Hey, we tried a woman and it didn't work. So now we are going back to hiring a guy." As if that one woman represented our entire gender. They won't just say, "It didn't work out with that one particular woman," which is what they say when a male coach fails.

When I first started coaching, I always had a man on my staff. Because of the men's network in coaching

Left to right: Carol Owens, Niele Ivey, Muffet McGraw, and Beth Morgan

(a lot of AAU coaches are men), I thought I would need a man on my staff to break into that group and help with recruiting. I also thought that it would be great to be a woman and have men work for me and to have my team see that. Later, we committed to an all-female staff. When we went to the Final Four, we realized we were picking up a lot of new fans because others thought it was important in women's basketball to have all women coaches. It was important to show others that an all-women staff could be just as successful as a staff with men.

HELP EACH OTHER
AND MOVE FORWARD

When I started coaching in college it was long after Title IX had passed. Title IX is a federal law that states that men's and women's athletics should have equal opportunities. It was pretty easy for universities to say, "Yes, we have given women opportunities," but where was the equal funding? The men were flying to places and women were taking the bus. The men were eating at nice restaurants and women were eating fast food. There were differences in days and times we were playing our games, with women's teams always getting the worse end. There were so many things that were unequal.

Although my own teams were not given the same financial backing as our men's teams, I decided not to say anything. I kept thinking that when we had some success I would speak up. Success means winning. I only spoke up after we started to win. That was wrong. What message did that send to the young women I was coaching? Do we have to reach a certain level of success before we can be treated equally? Of course not. But we have been socialized to accept things as they are and not to make waves. To get along and go along. To be in the background where we are not recognized and not heard.

I think about the recent presidential election. Here it was 2020 and we still hadn't elected a female president. During the primary process, when there were women candidates, the women were not treated the same as the male candidates. With the women, the discussion was about likability and electability. What about capability? Shouldn't women be judged by their performance and their resume just like men are? Instead, it seemed as if the women candidates were judged by their appearance and were described by words such as "sensitive" and "emotional." It's true that women have come a long way in national politics since women won the right to vote one hundred years ago, but I think we should expect more.

How do we spark change and create more opportunities for women? First, women need to empower other women. We need to help each other. We need to learn to network just like men do. Men can meet someone new and within five minutes they are figuring out how they can help each other. They discuss golf courses they can play on together and football games they might be able to hook up the other with tickets for. From there, they move on to discussions about business. On the other hand, it takes women five minutes together to decide if they even like each other, not if they can work together.

Men use their connections well while women are reluctant to do so.

Women need to stick up for each other. This rule should be in place in business, in college sports, and even down to lower levels of sports. I've heard mothers complain about their daughter's high school coach. They say things such as, "My daughter just doesn't respect a woman coach. A male coach always gets more out of her as a player." I am astonished that women could treat each other this way. Yes, the daughter's woman coach might not have been the right coach for that program, but that doesn't mean that another woman coach wouldn't get respect from her team.

Change starts with the attitude of each woman and each girl. When you hear someone stereotype women, take a moment to correct them. For women to be our best selves, change must take place in our attitudes toward ourselves and other women. We must support each other and work together to prove that women can be just as confident and competent as men, and just might bring something to the table that men cannot.

4.

ESTABLISH YOUR OWN VISION

I am the least introspective person you could ever meet. I don't spend a lot of time thinking about "where I want to be in five years." In fact, I always hated that question. But because it is your job as a leader to establish a vision for your program and where you want it to go, you do need a plan on how to get there. You need to answer questions about the definition of success and how you will go about achieving success.

When I first started coaching, I would go to a coaches' clinic and come home with all these new ideas that I was going to try. I was easily influenced by a coach who had success doing things a certain way. Whether it was this person's overall vision or something specific such as, a new defense or offense, I would think if I just copied what I heard at the clinic success would follow. Wrong!

It is a leader's job to have her own vision for her program or organization. Most times you will do this in collaboration with others; in my case as a college basketball coach, my vision had to fit in with the larger vision of my athletic department and my university. But when it came to our basketball program, it was up to me to establish my own vision because I was ultimately the one responsible for its success. For me, setting a vision began with examining essential core values. *What did I want my team to stand for?* I wanted my team to rely on the same core values that I relied on: accountability, honesty, integrity, and commitment to excellence. I expected my coaching staff and players to buy into these core values. These were core values that would lead our team to success.

My vision of success was always pretty simple. I wanted to win. Period. I learned that copying someone else's formula was not the best route to that result. My team had many variables that were different from the other coaches' teams. I was coaching at a different school, working for a different athletic director and university president, playing in a different conference, and the list goes on. I would have to do things my own way if my team was going to win.

So what goes into winning and success? Hiring the right staff, getting the right chemistry, is extremely

Muffet McGraw (center) with coaches Carol Owens (left) and Niele Ivey (right).

important. The assistants' job is to make the head coach's job easier. Choose them to fill in your weaknesses with their strengths. Everyone needs to complement each other, but you can't expect to agree at all times. You need diversity of thought. You need to have a staff that represents your team in their appearance, personality type, and background. The players need someone they can talk with based at least in part on what they have in common with the assistants.

While you can't all be the same, it is crucial for everyone to have a positive energy, intensity, competitiveness, and great worth ethic. Everything assistant coaches do—from how they conduct individual workouts with players, to their demeanor on the bench during games, to how they talk with recruits—has to reflect the cohesiveness of your staff and their confidence in you as a leader. One of the questions I would always ask myself when I hired an assistant was whether or not I would want to be around this person after a loss. I needed people around me who wanted to win as badly as me and who would want to do whatever it took to correct a defeat.

A BEGINNING STEP: ESTABLISH RULES THAT FIT YOUR CULTURE

Once you have your staff in place you can begin working on your team's culture. Culture is defined as the standards you expect everyone to live up to and that you will not bend on. Rules fit the culture by acting as a gauge for determining whether or not standards are being met. For example, one of our standards was timeliness, so we had specific rules about being on time for appointments and class. We also differentiated between being late and missing altogether. There were different consequences for both.

We also had very basic rules that had to do with not embarrassing yourself, our program, or the university. This meant we had rules about social media. I told our players to tweet as if the president of the university—a Catholic priest—was reading it. Bad language in a post, even using only initials, was prohibited. We had rules for behavior on the court and on the bench during games. We wanted players to always acknowledge the passer when they make a basket. Just a simple nod, smile, or pointing to the person who threw the pass was enough. If someone took a charge playing defense, all four players on the court were to run to her and help her up. This made the others recognize what a sacrifice their team-mate made for them and hopefully encouraged them to be the one to take the charge the next time. When

a player went to the free throw line, the other players huddled near her and touched each other's hands while in a circle. We also asked all players to stand when a teammate came out of the game. A lot of times I would play film of our time-out huddles and show them to the team. We commented on the players' body language and what I thought was inappropriate (for example, not paying attention, joking around, or pouting). I was big on rules and I wanted players to know what was expected of them in almost any situation that could arise.

Our standards were our core values—accountability, honesty, integrity, and a commitment to excellence. Without these we couldn't have reached our ultimate criteria for success, which was to win.

THE STANDARD OF ACCOUNTABILITY

To be accountable means answering for your words, actions, and decisions to others. As a coach, I was accountable for what happened on the basketball court. When things were not going well it was my responsibility to fix them. Many times I couldn't fix a problem that occurred in the game until we got to practice. At practice I could do several things to solve a problem while at the same time making the players and assistant coaches share responsibility for what had happened. In other words, everyone shared in the problem and everyone shared in the solution.

I had assistant coaches assigned to each position group: point guards, wings, and post players. If we had a discussion in our staff meeting about why the post players were not scoring enough, our assistant in charge of that group—Carol Owens—would say, "I will work with them more to increase their scoring production." But then an assistant for the guards (Niele Ivey or Beth Cunningham) might assert, "No, it's not your fault. Our point guards need to make better entry passes so the posts can catch and score."

The assistant coaches were taking responsibility. If your staff isn't accountable, how can you expect your players to be? My job was to make sure they fixed the problems at practice.

Similarly, I wouldn't let my assistants or players blame someone else for something that went wrong. And neither would I blame anyone else, including the referees. I would force our players to look at themselves and acknowledge they had control over what they did on the court. When I asked a player, "Who didn't box out?" she knew she needed to answer honestly because I would go to the film and find out. If she hadn't taken responsibility for her mistake she would be in even bigger trouble. I never wanted players who would blame a teammate by saying things such as, "She was in the wrong spot," or "She didn't set the screen." We all make plenty of mistakes so there shouldn't be a need to blame somebody else. My players also learned that when they made a bad play, if they looked over to me at the bench immediately to show they knew they were responsible, they would have a better chance of avoiding a stern look or stern words from me when I had the chance.

At practice, we had a way to record our accountability. Sometimes we would put up a flip chart—the old kind of scoreboard before there were electronic ones—and use it to keep track of mistakes. We would scrimmage four-on-four and count things such as not setting proper screens, giving up the middle on a drive, not being on the help side on defense, and more. It doesn't take talent or athletic ability to do those things correctly in a basketball game. Just effort. Every time a team would get to ten mistakes, the players had to run. I liked the flip chart because it was visible and everyone knew when they were getting closer to ten. It forced everyone to be accountable. Sometimes we would be even more strict and force our players to be perfect with no mistakes on every possession. I would assign one coach for each player to constantly watch her every move, and if it wasn't perfect she would be charged with a mistake and we would get to ten very quickly.

THE STANDARD OF HONESTY

I am always amazed that, after I speak on a panel or at an event, someone will come up to me afterward and say, "I really appreciate your candor" or "Thank you for being so honest." I've always tried to be honest and clearly speak the truth. I don't think there is any other way to be. I knew it was important to be honest with my players. I didn't lie to them during the recruiting process and I certainly didn't lie to them when I coached them.

When I was a younger coach, I might have been too honest. Some would say brutally honest. I would always be honest with a player when she was doing something wrong, and maybe not as honest as I should have been when she was doing something right. I eventually grew to take on the idea of the "one-minute manager," a popular concept that is based on catching people doing good things. I would apply this by sending a text or dropping a note in a player's locker when she did something well or when I felt she was losing confidence. A kind-spoken word is always appreciated, but when a player had something she could go back and read later it seemed to make a greater impact.

I agree with the adage "Praise in public and critique in private." No one should ever be embarrassed or demeaned in front of others. Sometimes this is hard to do. You need to have enough self-control and wait until you cool off before you speak with someone who has made a mistake. There were several games when we were losing at halftime that I wanted to go in the locker room and yell at my team. Or throw an eraser. But I rarely did those things. Instead, I would vent with my assistant coaches in the hallway outside. They had already heard a lot from me on the sideline during the first half and would usually vent along with me, although I was definitely the loudest. We would quickly move on from what had happened to how we could fix the problems. The assistants would focus on their own position groups. After I cooled off a bit, I found it much easier to address the whole team.

If you don't have a personal relationship with the people you manage, they will not accept your constant critique. I constantly individually critiqued players and did so honestly. They all knew that I wanted them to play hard on every possession, compete, and give their best effort. I wanted each player to reach her potential and I would not settle for anything less. The players knew these expectations. They knew that I believed in them. As head coach, my focus during practice was always on the starters and the top subs. But I couldn't forget about the rest of the team. Every player had a role and I made it a point to compliment the bench players for their positive energy, enthusiasm, and encouragement for their teammates.

There were also times when I would ask the players to rate their teammates on qualities such as competitiveness, work ethic, and desire to win. I would ask them who they would most like to be on the court with. Sometimes hearing critiques from their peers makes an even bigger impression than when it comes from the leader. I would receive the written critiques and then meet with each player in private. These were usually very honest conversations. I would show the player the critiques (but not tell her if she ranked near the bottom in a category). I would then ask the player where she would rate herself in each category and then explain what I thought about her and her teammates' evaluations.

Playing time is a big concern for players, just as being assigned or overlooked for a key project might be for an employee in another business setting. I would be very honest with players about playing time. I wanted them to know that they controlled how many minutes they got in a game. It was their job to work on their weaknesses as player. It was their job to improve so that they could contribute to the team's success. Sometimes I had to help players with their self-awareness about playing time. Maybe they weren't getting minutes because they happened to be playing behind an All-American. Or maybe it was because they just weren't putting in the work. I would pull them aside at practice and tell them what they needed to improve on. I would watch film with them and point out times when they did exactly what I was asking of them and when they didn't. I couldn't just tell a player she wasn't rebounding enough. I had to show her film clips of her retreating down the floor to get on offense when she should have been crashing the defensive boards. I would also suggest drills for her to get better. But ultimately it was the players' job to prove to me that they should be on the court.

THE STANDARD OF INTEGRITY

At Notre Dame, integrity matters. The school has a strong spiritual side. Faculty, staff, and students are joined in a common bond of caring that reflects the Catholic influence of the university. Although a majority of our players were not Catholic, that didn't change the fact that they were united through the spirit of Notre Dame, the mission of the university, and their own belief

in God. I always loved what Notre Dame's former president, Fr. Edward Malloy, once said, "Our campus is in South Bend, Indiana; our classroom is the world." Notre Dame has a broad reach everywhere in the world.

As leaders of a collegiate team, we were to follow the NCAA rules and report any possibility of infraction to our athletic department's compliance office. Most importantly, not only were we expected to follow the *letter* of the law, but the *intent* of the law as well. The university's expectations that its athletic programs are to be run with integrity made it easier to stress that same standard with my coaches and players. If you are going to work or play at Notre Dame, this is just the way it has to be.

The standard of integrity had concrete benefits for our players. We were always in the top five in student-athlete graduation success. In a ten-year period (2004–2014), we earned a perfect 100 percent NCAA Graduation Success Rate score. We had five different Academic All-Americans over the years. Two of them—Ruth Riley

Ruth Riley

television. We were embarrassed. How do you come back from that and win a national championship? I followed my rule and didn't say much to the team after the game. I went home and watched the film. When we came back to practice, I showed them a few clips, but the answer to why we played poorly was very simple: We didn't work. We didn't compete. We didn't try. That was not Notre Dame basketball.

For the rest of the season, even with the injuries, our team applied the lesson from the Louisville game very well. I thought it was amazing that we received a number one seed for the NCAA tournament. We had to travel all the way out west to play. We faced the University of Oregon, a very good team, in the regional finals and beat them to get to the Final Four. I thought that our team had overachieved just to get there. But obviously their standard of excellence was beyond just getting to the Final Four. They continued on and got two more wins, one over Connecticut, the tournament favorite, and a win in the national finals over Mississippi State University. In both games Arike Ogunbowale hit last-second shots to give us the wins.

Our roster was so depleted because of injury that the championship was not just improbable, it was amazing. At dinner with the team after beating Mississippi State, we went around the table and each person shared a few

and Carol Lally—are in the College Sports Information Directors of America Academic All-American Hall of Fame. The standard of integrity and these kinds of results always reminded my assistants and me that, in addition to being coaches, we were educators and teachers too.

Carol Lally

THE STANDARD OF A COMMITMENT TO EXCELLENCE

Our national championship in 2018 was tremendous improbable. Before the season even started, we lost All-American player to a torn anterior cruciate ligame (ACL). A couple of weeks later, one of our point guar also tore an ACL. By the time the NCAA tourname began we had a total of four players with ACL injuri including the back-up point guard who had replaced starter. We had more ACL tears than losses.

One of our losses that season was to University Louisville, 100 to 60. That's a forty-point loss, the wo in our program's history. The game was on natio of their favorite memories from the season. Our point guard, Marina Mabrey, said she loved looking over to the bench after making a mistake in the championship game, seeing me shaking my head looking down at the floor. She knew I couldn't take her out because we didn't have anyone else to replace her. And what if I did take her out after her fourth turnover? Then she wouldn't have been in the game to hit a huge three-pointer with 2:01 to go to pull us within two points of the lead. It was her first and only three-pointer of the game. I love when a player comes through like that in a pressure situation. It is a moment to celebrate. Marina (below) had the confidence to take a big shot. She will always be able to look

at herself and say, "I did it." I was happy she found out what she was capable of and maybe realized after the game why I had pushed her so hard.

This kind of individual and team excellence is what we expected of our players at Notre Dame. As part of our recruiting visits, we would have our legendary alumni association director, the late Chuck Lennon, meet with the recruits and their parents. He would always end his speech by saying, "If you want to be good—as a player and as a student—go someplace else. If you want to be *great*, come to Notre Dame." We wanted to be great and we wanted our players to strive for excellence in both academics and in basketball.

When I had a player who was committed to reaching her potential and was willing to work hard in order to achieve excellence, then my job was much easier. There are some players who want to be great but really don't know how to get there. And there are others who want it to be easy to reach their potential. It is the leader's job to work with all the kinds of people and figure out how to make them great. At Notre Dame, we did this in different ways: by challenging our players, motivating them, and inspiring them.

All I asked of players was to meet me halfway. If they wanted to play professional basketball in the WNBA, I would help them to reach that level. If they wanted to be conference player of the year or All-American, I wanted that too. We were at our best as a team when each player was playing at the highest level she could. Why wouldn't I want them to achieve personal greatness?

After each game, we recognized players who had season highs and career bests in certain statistical categories such as scoring, assists, or rebounding. But we also rewarded statistics such as field goal percentage and free throw percentage, because it wasn't about how many they scored but how effective they were for the number of shots taken. One thing that is hard to get through to players is that it's not all about scoring points. There are so many things that go into being an All-American and team success is at the top of the list. A player has to affect the game in more ways than one. She can't be one-dimensional. She has to be able to rebound, defend, and even have a positive assist-to-turnover ratio too.

But there is no doubt that to be an All-American, a player has to have one thing that she is *really* good at. A player having one special skill made a coaching decision easier. If we needed a defensive stop and I knew the player who could best do that, she was likely to get the call to go into the game and be assigned to the other team's top scorer. To be an All-American, statistics are, in fact, important. I didn't like to compare our players with players on other teams, but sometimes I would look at the stats of other great players and show our players what an All-American stat line should look like. This was another way for our players to measure what it would take to be great.

The standard of excellence was for all players, not just the great ones trying to move on to the WNBA. I always had certain players I just wanted to have in a game. They were chemistry players. They did all the little things necessary to help win a basketball game. They brought energy to defense, took charges, set good screens, and rebounded. Many of these things didn't show up in stat lines, but these types of players made vital contributions. No matter who the player is, all you want to do as a coach is to help them reach their potential and to be as good as they can be. Or, I should say, because it was Notre Dame, as *great* as they can be.

5.

SET YOUR FOUNDATION

You've established your culture, have a vision of where you want to go, and now you need to set the foundation of your team. For me, as a basketball coach, the foundation meant the players. The players were the ones who would have to form the culture and make our vision a reality through their success. The biggest lesson I learned in recruiting players was that how well a player would "fit" in the program and contribute to the team's chemistry was more important than her talent. I started by asking myself "Is this someone I would want to be around for four years? Am I going to enjoy coaching her?" I would answer those questions by taking a closer look at things beyond what a stat line might reveal.

First, I looked at how competitive she was and what kind of leader she was. Then, I would go deeper, asking: How do her teammates treat her? Does she make her teammates better? Do they look to her when the game is close? Does she encourage them when they make a mistake or does she roll her eyes and look up in the stands at her parents? Does she make eye contact with her coach? My assistants have gone to see a recruit play and said, "She's really good, but you aren't going to want to coach her." And that was the end of that recruit.

I loved coaching and wanted it to be enjoyable. I tried to surround myself with players who were competitive, hard-working, self-motivated, and who could get along with others. You can teach almost anything else, but you can't teach those things.

Of course, when we were recruiting we also looked for players with certain basketball skills that matched up with the way we wanted to play. When I first started coaching, women's basketball was all about defense. Half-court offenses were more popular. Teams tried to limit offensive possessions while holding the other team to fewer points. But as time went on, I really wanted a team that played up-tempo and could score. I stopped looking for that one-dimensional defender and started looking for players with a better and more varied skill set.

Once you have developed the system for your team, you can decide what kind of people fit into it. But remember: There is something more important than the skills a person has in doing any job: how she fits into your group's culture. Harry Perretta, the former Villanova University coach, once told me that he only recruited players he could get along with—for 335 days of the year he could be happy with them because on the other thirty game days he might not be.

SETTING TEAM GOALS

Coaches know the potential of their teams. Sometimes you know you have a chance to win the conference and get into the NCAA tournament. Sometimes you have a team with Sweet 16 or Final Four potential. And there are other years when you are rebuilding. No matter what your team's potential, you have to set some daily goals that connect to your larger goals for the season.

We always had a team meeting early in the summer where I let the players decide what our team goals would be for the year. Everyone had a voice and free reign to mention whatever goals they wanted. This gave players a more personal stake in our team. We tried to have many season goals, such as, being undefeated at home, winning the regular season conference championship, winning the conference tournament, and winning the national championship.

Setting those types of goals worked over several seasons, but my last team, in 2019–20, was facing a rebuilding year. I made a mistake that year by letting the players set big goals, such as "winning the conference," even though I realized we didn't have the team to do it. None of our returning players had played more than a few minutes in the Final Four the previous year and, because our graduated players who did play had made it look easy, they assumed that type of success would happen again. My goal was to finish in the top four of the conference and make the NCAA tournament. I didn't even think we would be seeded high enough to host a first round NCAA tournament game. I didn't want to

Notre Dame Fighting Irish 2019–2020

burst the balloon of our players who had set higher goals, but in hindsight I probably should have.

TRACKING TEAM GOALS

Once our team set their season goals, we had ten statistical goals we tried to accomplish in every game. These were goals related to statistics such as field goal percentage, points allowed, rebound margin, assist-to-turnover ratio, forced turnovers, and steals. It was rare that we would accomplish seven out of ten goals in any game, but I wanted to aim high and I always expected more from the team.

We also had daily goals that would help us to reach our season goals. We talked about daily effort, holding ourselves and our teammates to a higher standard, studying scouting reports, and competing every day to make each other better. These types of goals were harder to measure, but speaking them out loud gave me a reference point at the end of practice to point to and tell the team whether or not I thought they achieved their goals for the day. The more you allow anyone you supervise to set the daily goals, the easier it is to remind them of what they said they wanted to accomplish long-term. Getting players to hold themselves and their teammates to the daily goals took great leadership from our captains and our best players. We were fortunate that our best players were always our hardest workers too.

The one place a coach can't control by setting goals (or any other means, really) is the locker room. That is why recruiting to fit your culture is so important. The seniors and other team leaders control the locker room. You need to trust them to do their job. You can, however, monitor the mood of the team by meeting with your captains on a weekly basis to get a report on how things are going when you aren't around. We allowed our players to choose our captains, but made sure there was some diversity among them. You don't want all the captains to think alike. You need different personalities so that one captain can function as "bad cop" at times and another captain can be more of the encouraging type.

PUTTING THE PLAN INTO PRACTICE

Designing my practice schedule for the season was one of my favorite parts of my job. I used a notebook to track the entire season. I liked to write things out in detail so that I didn't miss anything, but I always wrote in pencil because things did change. The date of the first game of the season was always starred. I made a list of everything that had to be taught at practice and learned by the players before the first game. Then I began writing out the plans for each practice.

There are two basic parts to playing basketball (and most other sports): offense and defense. I had a list of progressions for man-to-man defense. For offense, we had to start by teaching the proper way to set and use screens before we could proceed. There were several variations of our offense to teach. I think one of the hardest things for a basketball coach to decide is what you will run on offense, that is, what type of offense will fit your team. It's great if you can recruit to your system. I wanted to have women who got up and down the floor

and played up-tempo. But you don't always get the types of players that fit your offense to a T and you have to be flexible.

Planning can be hard at the beginning of a season because you aren't yet sure which of your new players will be able to step up and make big plays. Also, you can't plan on your offense running through just one person. What if she gets injured? My thought was to always incorporate some quick-hitting plays in the offense for different players so that we could always be prepared for the unexpected. You don't have to have everything in place by the first game either. We had some things ready for the nonconference portion of the schedule, then added some more things for the conference games, and put in even more wrinkles to both our offense and defense in time for the NCAA tournament. Up until the NCAA tournament, we were working on getting better. In March Madness, it was all about winning.

I met with the staff every day to work on the upcoming practice plan and to reflect on the previous practice and how we thought things were going. It was important to have that time together so that we were all on the same page. We would usually move the meeting out of the office and onto the court so that we could demonstrate our drills and new plays so that all the coaches would be comfortable breaking down and explaining them if a player had a question.

ATTENTION TO DETAIL

Creating your vision, setting your goals, and crafting a plan to get there are really only the beginning parts of the process. To have success you must remain relentless in attending to the details of building on everything you have previously set up. You can't become complacent and you can't let your staff and team get away with not giving their best effort every day.

Attention to detail in all aspects of your vision and plan is crucial. Our coaching staff expected the players to go for perfection in every drill. There were times we would play a game called "perfect offense" where the players would have to execute five different plays that met these criteria: no turnovers, three rebounders in the lane, and one player getting back on defense. They had to score on three out of five of the possessions and couldn't run the same play twice. All of the cuts and screens had to be perfect too. Coach's judgment. Sometimes this drill would take thirty minutes for them to succeed. Other times we had to lower the bar and just go for three perfect plays in a row.

Any leader will have setbacks, and there will always be parts of your plan you try with those you supervise that just don't seem to work. At that point, it's simply wise to stop repeating those things that are causing frustration and continue with some other part of your plan that does work well. I do think it's important that you don't deviate too far from your plan and risk the team thinking you have lost confidence in what you are doing. You have to believe in your plan and be resilient and steadfast in your approach. You can't only look ahead to the final results—wins versus losses—but rather, you should look for improvement and growth both in individuals and your team as whole.

If we had a game where we were bad in a certain area, either on offense or defense, I would go back in my practice notebook and see if the team had worked on that particular area enough. Usually I would find that it was my fault that we hadn't spent enough time on what had gone wrong in the game at practice. That's another reason why I kept my practice plans in a notebook rather than typing them out on a sheet each day. A notebook was much easier for reference.

In fact, I saved my practice notebooks from year to year. There were always some similarities between my current team and a past team. I also kept a journal with my practice notebook that reminded me that when I was thinking "we have never played this bad before," we had in another season. It was good to be able to go back and remember what I had been thinking at certain points in previous seasons while knowing how it had all worked out.

LEARNING FROM OTHERS

One of the things I loved about the coaching profession was how everyone was willing to share what they were doing, often in clinics and seminars. But what I really loved and appreciated was sitting in a gym and watching games with other coaches and talking with them about things such as how they ran their offense or how they expected their players to guard. I never missed a chance to talk with other coaches. I remember when I was introduced to Chicago Bulls coach Tom Thibodeau on the sideline of a Notre Dame football game. I immediately launched into basketball questions with him. When the Bulls and Indianapolis Pacers played an exhibition game one year at Notre Dame, I was amazed that the coaches on both teams were willing to answer any questions that I had for them.

You learn so much from others. I was always surprised that more coaches didn't reach out to their counterparts and watch other teams practice. I found it helpful to compare my process to what other coaches were doing to see what changes I might make. When we started running the Princeton motion offense, I spent time going to practices of teams that had been using that offense for a while and talking with their coaches. Similarly, when we went to the Bulls's famous triangle offense years ago,

I was able to watch the Bulls practice and talk with the architect of the triangle, Tex Winter. One year, our entire staff went to see the Detroit Pistons practice at the invitation of Stan Van Gundy. Next we visited John Beilein at the University of Michigan and learned about the 1-3-1 defense. Then we went over to East Lansing to watch Tom

Muffet McGraw with University of North Carolina coach Roy Williams

Izzo and Michigan State University's team. What a great day of triple workouts! In my final year of coaching, I was able to spend time with Brad Stevens, coach of the Boston Celtics, and watch his team over a couple of days. I loved getting new ideas about everything from drills to out-of-bounds plays to fuller offensive sets.

It's critical to keep an open mind to new ideas. Sometimes when we have done something the same way for years, we are hesitant to change. Drills and practices can get stale if you don't add some variations. You don't have to be swayed by everything you see from other teams and coaches and you have to make sure anything new you want to implement will fit your players and your style of play. Whenever I added new assistant coaches to the staff, they were also able to add fresh ideas and new perspectives.

I think, in general, women leaders need to look for more opportunities to connect with other leaders in the same profession. It isn't that hard to do. In basketball, when teams come in to play a men's game at their school, it's easy for a women's coach to ask the opposing men's coach if they can watch his team's shoot-around. When you are out on the road recruiting, you can always check to see if there is a college team practicing nearby that you could go and watch. The specific ways of reaching out to colleagues in other professions may differ, but the principles and value are the same.

Women are sometimes afraid that they won't appear as confident if they go around asking what others in their field are doing. I think it's just the opposite. You show your confidence by acknowledging that you don't know everything and that you are willing to learn.

6.

STAND UP
FOR YOURSELF

I was asked a question at the Final Four press conference in 2019 after we had just defeated Connecticut: "How seriously do you take being 'that voice' standing up for women in college basketball?" I took my answer a bit further than expected, to say the least! I started out: "Did you know that the Equal Rights Amendment was introduced in 1967 and it still hasn't passed? We need thirty-eight states to agree that discrimination on the basis of sex is unconstitutional."

The words poured from my heart, probably after decades of frustration with the lack of women in leadership in all areas, not merely in women's basketball. I talked for a full two minutes. I mentioned the huge disparity between men and women in leadership. I pointed out that less than 5 percent of CEOs in Fortune 500

companies are women. (It wasn't until early in 2020 that all Fortune 500 companies had at least one woman on their boards.)

"I'm getting tired of the novelty of the first female governor of this state, the first female African American mayor of this city," I said. "When is it gonna become the norm instead of the exception? How are these young women looking up and seeing someone that looks like them preparing them for the future?" I strongly made my point that we don't have enough visible women leaders. We don't have enough women in power.

The response I received was amazing. It was a message that resonated across the country because it was something that everyone needed to hear. The video of my answer was retweeted thousands of times, including by Barack Obama, Billie Jean King, and Hillary Clinton. I heard from women in many different industries, all of whom shared that they were in a male-dominated business with few, if any, female role models to look up to. It wasn't just women who responded to what I said;

I got dozens of letters from fathers who described how they had clearly witnessed their daughters being treated differently in school and in sports than their sons were. I was disappointed, however, that I didn't hear from more female women's basketball coaches about what I had said.

So many women head coaches hire men on their staff when there are countless women who are as qualified, if not more so. Men coaching women's teams also hire other men as assistants. I don't understand this. Young women need to be able to learn from and talk with someone who has gone through some of the same things they are going through. It's impossible for a man to understand sexism when he has never experienced it. Men *can* be role models of character, mentors, and skill instructors for women. But they can't teach women how to find their voices in a male-dominated workplace and world. Men can't show women how to lead like a woman. This is why we need more female role models and why I wished I had heard from more women coaches after my Final Four press conference.

HELP TO ADVANCE
OTHER WOMEN

Women most often work in male-dominated industries. Whether in athletics, law, medicine, education, retail, or any other industry, women all go through many of the same frustrations with subtle sexism in the workplace. We don't get promoted at the same rate as men. We often don't even get interviewed for a promotion while we watch someone less qualified move past us.

When someone in an organization is in a position to hire and is asked about whether or not the position will go to a woman, the answer is always the same: "I will hire the most qualified person for the job." As if that person wouldn't normally be a woman! Of course the most qualified person should be hired. I just want employers to look harder at the females in the applicant pool. And because women don't network with other women the way men do, an employer will need to be more aggressive in seeking out qualified women candidates.

The first place to look is always within the employer's own organization. Women should be prepared sufficiently for management positions so that when an opportunity for advancement opens up, they will be ready. Women should talk with their supervisors and get regular evaluations of their work. They should ask not only about how they are doing but how they can improve. Does your supervisor know you are interested in being promoted? Don't assume anything.

The "old boys' network" is still going strong. How can women break it up or compete against it? We need a better network of women helping women. We need to use our connections and ask for help from other women. If we are in a position of power, we need to reach back and pull more women up with us. Women are great at

Muffet McGraw celebrates with Notre Dame director of athletics, Jack Swarbrick.

networking when they are trying to get their kids on the right soccer team or a ride to school. So why not use those same skills for when you are trying to break into or move up in a profession?

We also need men to advocate for us. We have to find someone who already has a seat at the table. In most cases this is a man. Use some of the men you know as a resource for how to get hired or get promoted. Men can be a mentor for you, but they also have to be willing to make a strong recommendation for you because it is usually another man who is doing the hiring. If you can't find someone to advocate for you, then you need to speak up even louder for yourself. If you are a woman of color, you may have to outright shout to be heard. And when another woman does succeed, be happy about it. Her success helps us all.

NEVER UNDERSELL YOURSELF

When the coronavirus outbreak hit in early 2020, some of the countries that handled it best were led by women. I am thinking especially of New Zealand where forty-year-old Jacinda Ardern was described by *Atlantic* magazine as "the most effective leader on the planet." There have been other prominent women leaders in recent times: Malala Yousafzai was the youngest recipient of the Nobel

Peace Prize after standing up against the Taliban, and who can forget Swedish climate activist Greta Thunberg who gave an impassioned address at the United Nations Climate Change Conference in 2018 when she was only fifteen years old? If these young women can stand up on the world stage and speak out for what is right, then I think all women should be able to do more.

Women need to fight harder for what they want, but first they have to identify what exactly it is they want. Do you want to lead an organization or are you happy in your current role? Some women (and men) prefer creating meaning and success within non-leadership positions. I am thinking of schoolteachers who

Malala Yousafzai

Greta Thunberg

do not want to rise in administration positions because they prefer the daily interactions with students. Some assistant coaches in basketball and other sports remain assistants for very similar reasons. There are many other positive reasons for not seeking out leadership positions.

However, you should never back away from a promotion because you question your own ability. Very often the people that get positions of leadership are not the most qualified but rather are those who sell themselves the best. Similarly, I've seen statistics that say that men ask for a raise about four times more often than women. And when we do negotiate, we always ask for less! We definitely undersell ourselves in almost every way. Men overpromise. We undervalue. You should learn instead to exude confidence and convince employers that you are the best person for the job or that you deserve a raise. Toot your own horn! If you don't stand up for yourself, who will?

EXPERIENCING GENDER ROLES AT AN EARLY AGE

What better place is there than sports to teach women about leadership? But the lessons have to start early. When young girls start playing sports, they almost always see only men in positions of leadership. We need women coaches, women referees, and women league officials to be witnesses to young girls from the time they first begin to play organized sports. Think about it. When

girls first start playing soccer or basketball at age five all the way up to elementary school, who is coaching the teams? It's almost always a man, usually someone's dad. Elite AAU travel teams are also dominated by male coaches and so are high school sports. I coached many players at Notre Dame for whom I was their first female head coach. The same structure is in place for referees and others in authority in athletics. They are typically men too.

Even at home, jobs often remain divided traditionally between women and men. I think the millennial generation will remove a lot of these stereotypes, but until then we need to be vigilant and not conform to preconceived roles. The bulk of the responsibility for raising kids still falls to women. Women organize carpools, pack lunches, cook dinners, and keep the house clean, though there are many exceptions to this. I was fortunate enough to marry a man who is one of the exceptions! One of the best things about being a working mom was that my son Murphy grew up without any preconceived ideas about gender roles in our family. I remember when Murphy came home from his first sleepover. He said, "Mom, wait until you hear this . . . his mom cooks!" When Murphy would come on road trips with our team, he was surrounded by very confident women and learned to appreciate and respect them. Because I often had to miss going to watch Murphy play in his own games, he learned a very healthy lesson in those instances too: the world didn't revolve around him.

Left to right: Francesca, Matt, Muffet, and Murphy McGraw.

Gender roles start at birth. Boys are blue and girls are pink. Boys can wrestle with each other, climb trees, and get dirty playing outside. Boys use sarcasm and razz each other. Boys learn about failing earlier in their lives than girls do. Boys learn to pick themselves up and move on to the next thing. Girls are more protected and not encouraged to be bold and take risks. Girls learn to be more sensitive and expect to be treated with more care so their feelings don't get bruised. How many times have you heard about girls having drama-laced fallings-out with friends? Yet boys have plenty of ups and downs with their friends and move through their childhoods for the most part without getting their feelings hurt. Girls need to learn how to battle adversity in the same way as boys.

Sports can help to build mental toughness for every player, boy or girl. I had a player once say at a team meeting that "everyone knows that if you come to Notre Dame and play for Coach McGraw you need to be mentally tough." I had to smile at that. Yes, I was tough. I was demanding. I taught demanding lessons that would stay with my players throughout their lives. I gave them both mental and physical challenges to overcome. That is why I tried to make our practices harder than the games. I wanted my players to go into a game and think it was easier because they were prepared. In the same way, I wanted them to go out into the world after Notre Dame knowing they were mentally prepared to meet any challenge.

TAKING PERSONAL RESPONSIBILITY

Girls need to learn the lesson of failure just like boys do. A lot of the success of this lesson depends on parents. Parents should never try and protect their kids from failing. Parents shouldn't try and fix every problem their kids have, such as not being the star of a team or not getting enough playing time. When kids face these types of issues on their own, they learn that not everyone can be the MVP, nor is playing time doled out evenly in the same way that participation ribbons are. A great lesson to learn early on is that life isn't fair and that you should stop expecting it to be. While you should never stop working hard to achieve what you want, you do need to learn that you don't always get what you want.

We have become a society of blamers. Parents have a big responsibility in making sure their kids take responsibility for their own successes and failures. Today, many parents teach their kids that nothing they do wrong is their own fault. This attitude extends into adulthood. How often have you heard a CEO or a politician come out and say, "I made a mistake. I take responsibility and I am going to fix what I did"? That rarely happens. How can we expect people to take responsibility for themselves and be accountable for their actions when those in leadership positions don't model what that looks like? In the spur of the moment, you might think it's easier to blame someone else for a mistake that you made, but that isn't beneficial for the long-term. It's better to learn skills early in life that teach you to battle through adversity rather than relying on dad or mom to fix every problem. And it's always best for parents to resist being the snowplow that clears all the obstacles from their child's path rather than teach them to be resilient and persistent through failure.

I always looked for players who had mental toughness—the ones who could handle situations when things didn't go their way. There were kids that we started to recruit and then noticed that they attended more than one high school and frequently changed their AAU teams. There are certainly some legitimate reasons why someone would change schools or even teams, but when we looked deeper at the pattern we often found parents at the root of the issue telling their daughters they should go somewhere else because they weren't getting what they wanted. That pattern often repeats itself in college. Some recruited players have one foot out the door before they even arrive on campus. I actually had a dad tell me once that he had let his daughter know, "If Notre

Dame doesn't work out, you can always leave." To no one's surprise, his daughter eventually did transfer out of our program.

For some players, college is the first time they aren't a starter or their team's best player. I always told my players that I didn't want to talk with their parents about their playing time, but I would talk with them about any issues they were having away from basketball. I also encouraged the parents that if their daughters called home to complain about anything basketball-related, they should send her back to me. The players already knew what my expectations were for them, meaning they knew why they weren't playing but were afraid to tell their parents the actual reasons.

I was fortunate to have so many supportive parents as part of our program over the years. Of course, we chose to recruit those types of parents. I was always grateful when parents could step back and let their daughters grow into amazing women by letting them become independent thinkers and letting them work through problems on their own. It's tough for parents to watch someone they love struggle. All parents hate to see their children experience tough times. But the smart parents are the ones who can find a balance of how to love and support their daughter without fighting her battles, and thus give her the tools to succeed on her own. They praise their daughter's team-first attitude and let her know how well she is doing as a good teammate and role model for others. One of the best things someone can say about you is that you were a great teammate.

WHERE DO WE
GO FROM HERE?

So how do we spark change in the area of women in leadership? I always tell my players that "Change starts with you!" In 2014 our team wore "I Can't Breathe" t-shirts during warmups before a game against the University of Michigan. It was the idea of one of our players to draw attention to the last words of Eric Garner, an African American man who died after being placed in a chokehold by New York City police during an arrest.

When asked after the game about our team's making such a statement, I told the media how proud I was of the players and reminded them that basketball is just a game; the lessons that women learned on our team were intended to help them to stand up for themselves in life after they were done playing. I'm glad I had players that were not afraid to use their voice and take a stand against injustice.

As a leader, you need to stand up for justice and teach those you lead to use their voices and their platform to make a difference. Also, you will deal with a diverse group of people. You will need to have empathy and understand what they are going through. It is essential to ask them questions and really listen to their answers. You won't be able to shy away from the tough conversations. As a leader, you will hear about problems and other bad things. Part of your job will be to reach out and help to solve those problems so that the individuals and the group itself can move forward.

Though styles of leadership differ, there is a general moral compass that works for any leader. Treat others as you wish to be treated. The greatest unhappiness in life comes when we compare ourselves to others. The only person you have to please is the one looking back at you in the mirror. If you have done your best and treated others with the same respect that you demand, that is all you can control.

So why aren't there more women in power? Because we are holding ourselves back! This isn't the senior prom. Stop waiting to be asked. You don't need anyone's permission to reach the top. If you want to be heard, speak up. If you want respect, command it. If you want the job, go for it. Stop waiting around for someone to notice you. What's the worst thing that can happen to you if you step up to lead? I think about what I would tell my team: "We may lose the game but we are going down swinging."

When it's all said and done, the best thing you can say about how you lived your life is that you did it with no regrets.

MUFFET McGRAW retired in 2020 after thirty-three years as head coach of the University of Notre Dame women's basketball team. With an overall record of 936-293, she led the Irish to two national championships (2001, 2018). McGraw's teams appeared in twenty-six NCAA tournaments, including seventeen Sweet Sixteens, nine Final Fours, and seven championship games.

Among her many honors, McGraw ranks first on the all-time wins list among single-sport coaches in the history of Notre Dame athletics. She is a three-time consensus NCAA coach of the year and a seven-time conference coach of the year. In 2017, McGraw was inducted into the Naismith Memorial Basketball Hall of Fame—the thirty-second woman member and thirteenth female coach. She received the 2017 Legends of Coaching Award from the John R. Wooden award committee.

A native of West Chester, Pennsylvania, McGraw earned her bachelor's degree in sociology from Saint Joseph's University in 1977.

McGraw and her husband Matt live in Granger, Indiana. They have a son, Murphy, and a daughter-in-law, Francesca.

AVE
AVE MARIA PRESS

Founded in 1865, Ave Maria Press,
a ministry of the Congregation of
Holy Cross, is a Catholic publishing
company that serves the spiritual and
formative needs of the Church and its
schools, institutions, and ministers;
Christian individuals and families; and
others seeking spiritual nourishment.

For a complete listing of titles from

Ave Maria Press

Sorin Books

Forest of Peace

Christian Classics

visit www.avemariapress.com

AVE MARIA PRESS
Notre Dame, IN
A Ministry of the United States Province of Holy Cross